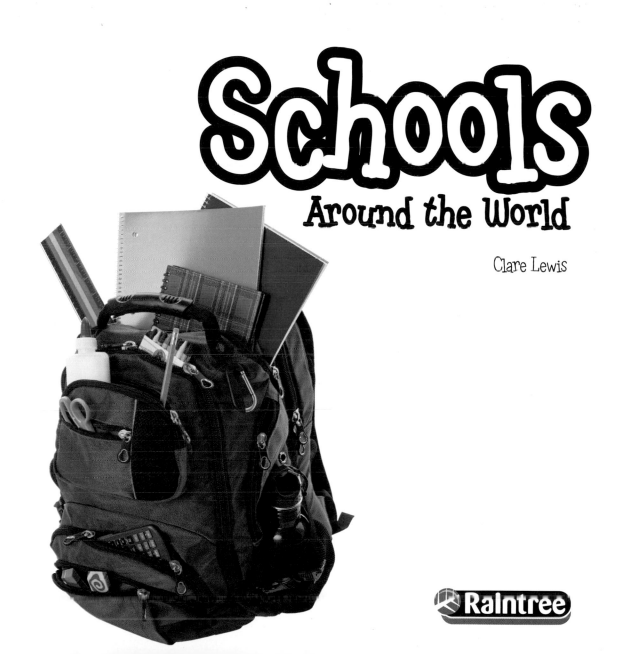

# Schools

## Around the World

Clare Lewis

**Raintree**

Raintree is an imprint of Capstone Global Library Limited, a company incorporated in England and Wales having its registered office at 7 Pilgrim Street, London, EC4V 6LB – Registered company number: 6695582

www.raintreepublishers.co.uk
myorders@raintreepublishers.co.uk

Edited by Joanna Issa, Shelly Lyons, Diyan Leake and Helen Cox Cannons
Designed by Cynthia Akiyoshi
Original illustrations © Capstone Global Library Ltd 2014
Picture research by Elizabeth Alexander and Tracy Cummins
Production by Victoria Fitzgerald
Originated by Capstone Global Library Ltd
Printed and bound in China

ISBN 978 1 406 28196 5
18  17  16  15  14
10 9 8 7 6 5 4 3 2 1

**British Library Cataloguing in Publication Data**
A full catalogue record for this book is available from the British Library.

**Acknowledgements**
We would like to thank the following for permission to reproduce photographs: Alamy pp. 8 & 22d (© Steve Morgan), 10 (© Jochen Tack), 11 & 23b (both © Bill Bachman), 14 (© Robert Harding Picture Library Ltd); Corbis pp. 9 & 22c (both © David Bathgate), 12 (© Ocean), 21 (© Ian Lishman/Juice Images); Getty Images pp. 5 (David Leahy), 6 & 22a (both UIG), 16 (NOAH SEELAM/AFP), 17 (StockLite), 18 (Chris Schmidt), 19 (Shannon Fagan); Shutterstock pp. 1 (© Brenda Carson), 2 (© Kozini), 3 (© JasonCPhoto), 15 (© Hurst Photo), 20 & 22e (both © Dmitry Berkut); Superstock pp. 4 (Exotica im / Exotica), 7 (Stock Connection), 13 & 22b (both Biosphoto), 23a (Stock Connection).

Cover photograph of Buddhist monks in a classroom in Sri Lanka reproduced with permission of Superstock (Cusp). Back cover photograph reproduced with permission of Shutterstock (© Hurst Photo).

Every effort has been made to contact copyright holders of material reproduced in this book. Any omissions will be rectified in subsequent printings if notice is given to the publisher.

All the internet addresses (URLs) given in this book were valid at the time of going to press. However, due to the dynamic nature of the Internet, some addresses may have changed, or sites may have changed or ceased to exist since publication. While the author and publisher regret any inconvenience this may cause readers, no responsibility for any such changes can be accepted by either the author or the publisher.

# Contents

# Schools everywhere

Children go to school all over the world.

Children go to school to learn.

# Different types of schools

Some schools are in cities.

Some schools are in the
countryside.

Some schools are outside.

This school is on a boat.

Some schools are at home.

Some children talk to their teachers
on the internet.

# How do children get to school?

Some children go to school on
a bicycle.

Some children walk to school.

Some children go to school on
a boat.

Some children go to school on
a bus.

# What do children learn at school?

Children learn to read and write.

Children learn to do maths.

Children learn about other countries.
Children learn about art and music.

# What else do children do at school?

Children meet their friends at school.

Children eat at school.

Schools are different all over
the world.

What do you like to do at school?

# Map of schools around the world

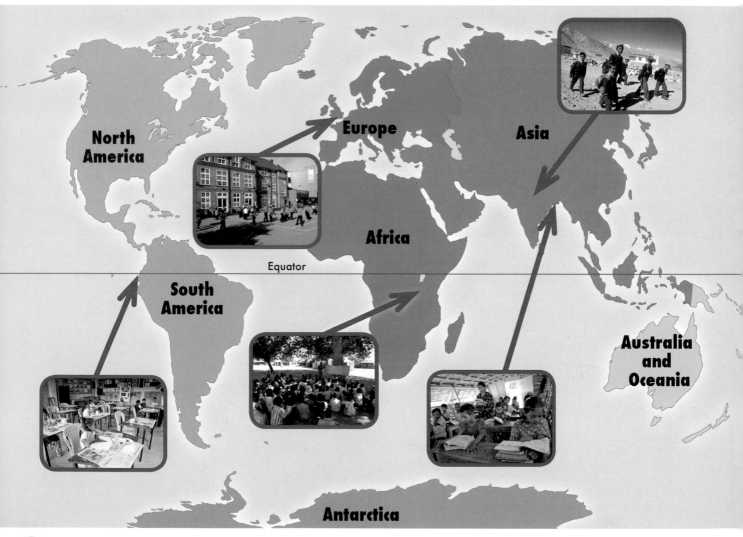

North America

Europe

Asia

Africa

Equator

South America

Australia and Oceania

Antarctica

# Picture glossary

**countryside** places that are away from towns and cities

**internet** way of using computers that allows people who are far away to share information

# Index

**Notes for parents and teachers**
**Before reading**

Ask children why they think they go to school. Ask them if they have ever been to any other schools before. What things were similar? What things were different? Show children a globe or map of the world and identify the continents. Explain that children go to school all over the world, and ask them to think about how schools in the book are similar and different as they read the book.

**After reading**

- Review pages 12–15 about how children get to school. Ask children how they got to school today and make a class graph to record and compare the different ways.

- Point out the map on page 22 and identify the continents with children. Demonstrate how to use the map to identify the continent on which different photos from the book were taken. Ask children where the photo on page 9 was taken (Asia). Have children look at the photo and discuss or list what things are similar and different between that school and their school.

Note on picture on page 12: NEVER ride a bicycle without a helmet.